Sex Positions

The Ultimate Guide for Exploding Couple's Sex Life with The Top Sex Positions

Bambi Colt

© **Copyright 2017 By Bambi Colt**

All rights reserved.

This document is geared towards providing exact and reliable information in regards to the topic and issue covered. The publication is sold with the idea that the publisher is not required to render an accounting, officially permitted, or otherwise, qualified services. If advice is necessary, legal or professional, a practiced individual in the profession should be ordered.

From a Declaration of Principles which was accepted and approved equally by a Committee of the American Bar Association and a Committee of Publishers and Associations.

In no way is it legal to reproduce, duplicate, or transmit any part of this document by either electronic means or in printed format. Recording of this publication is strictly prohibited, and any storage of this document is not allowed unless with written permission from the publisher. All rights reserved.

The information provided herein is stated to be truthful and consistent, in that any liability, regarding inattention or otherwise, by any usage or abuse of any policies, processes, or directions contained within is the solitary and utter responsibility of the recipient reader. Under no circumstances will any legal responsibility or blame be held against the publisher for any reparation, damages, or monetary loss due to the information herein, either directly or indirectly.

Respective authors own all copyrights not held by the publisher.

The information herein is offered for informational purposes solely and is universal as so. The presentation of the information is without a contract or any type of guarantee assurance.

The trademarks that are used are without any consent, and the publication of the trademark is without permission or backing by the trademark owner. All trademarks and brands in this book are for clarification and are the property of the owners themselves, not affiliated with this document.

Table of Content

Introduction..5

Chapter 1: Intimacy 1

Chapter 2: Romance 5

Chapter 3: Different Types of Positions 9

Chapter 4: Sensual Positions...................................13

Chapter 5: Spicy Positions 35

Chapter 6: Beyond the Bedroom.............................55

Conclusion

Introduction

"*Sex Positions:* The Ultimate Guide for Exploding Couple's Sex Life with The Top Sex Positions" is a book designed to help you bring romance back into your relationship. Unlike Kama Sutra-style books, this book is going to emphasize on actions and positions that can easily be completed by anyone, regardless of your flexibility or mobility.

The idea is to bring romance back into the everyday relationship, allowing you to obtain greater enjoyment and fulfillment from your relationship with your partner.

At one time or another, you likely had a fiery sex life with your partner, but over time it slowly dwindles as relationships settle in and people become comfortable with one another.

Alternatively, you may be fresh in a relationship and are seeking out advice on how to have a strong sex life from the get go. Regardless of where you are in experience and in life, this book can help you experience great joy in your sex life.

If you are ready to level up your experience and add fiery passion and romance to your relationship, then you have come to the right place. This book will provide you with excellent advice for both inside and outside of the bedroom, as well as some awesome new sex positions for you to try. Altogether, you will have everything you need to spark fierce and romantic passion in your relationship once again.

Chapter 1

Intimacy

In relationships, intimacy may come naturally, or it may take effort. Regardless of whether it's one way or the other is unimportant, the important part is that you realize the value of intimacy and what it adds to your relationship. By understanding the importance of intimacy, you can begin to take control over your relationship and ensure that your relationship flourishes with it.

The Importance of Intimacy

According to psychologists, a relationship that lacks intimacy will fail to thrive and will ultimately end up with two unhappy parties, likely separated, divorced, or otherwise split up. The importance of intimacy runs deep, as it is specifically the intimate connection between two people who are in love. You can have love without intimacy, but you cannot have a romantic relationship without intimacy. There may be periods where intimacy waxes and wanes, but overall the intimacy should always be present or in the very close background of a relationship. When the intimacy starts to die down, it is always a good idea to put in a little extra effort to bring it back up.

Different Types of Intimacy

You might be surprised, but there are different types of intimacy in relationships. The two primary types of intimacy are physical and emotional. Because of this, different partners are likely to see different types of intimacy as more important. You and your partner might have two different ideas of what intimacy should look like in your relationship, so it is important that you learn to communicate with these types of things.

Physical intimacy is an intimacy that is shown through physical touch. People who are more interested in physical intimacy tend to feel more connected to their partner through touch.

The touch can be non-sexual such as hand-holding, a hand on the shoulder, hugging, and even sitting next to each other with body parts touching. Or, it can be sexual. When you want to turn someone on who is more interested in physical intimacy, you need to use this to your advantage. Use sensual touching of various areas of the body as an opportunity to turn them on.

Emotional intimacy is an intimacy that is given and received through feelings. People who are more interested in emotional intimacy are turned on through words and other things that evoke emotions.

They may be more likely to respond to surprises, storytelling, gifts, and more.

Most relationships rely on both types of intimacy, though the balance will be unique to each individual relationship. Finding the perfect balance will require communication and practice as you both learn how to physically and emotionally communicate with each other in a way that nurtures your relationship.

Chapter 2

Romance

Romance stems from intimacy, as it is ultimately an extension of the intimacy itself. When there is intimacy in a relationship, you can be certain that some level of romance will prevail. If you want to have a really exciting sex life, you will want to build a solid foundation of intimacy and frost it off with a healthy helping of romance. Regardless of what someone's intimacy preference is, they will most certainly want to experience romance in their life. You can decide how you will display romance based on their preference for types of intimacy.

For Physical People

Anyone who likes physical intimacy will want to experience acts of romance in the physical sense. There are many ways that you can be romantic towards someone physically. When you are physically romantic, you want to do so with both sexual and non-sexual intentions. What that means is that while sometimes you are going to want to allow the romance to lead towards sex, you should not always allow for it to go that far. When you use physical intimacy to result in sex every single time, it can actually break down the value of this type of intimacy as your partner will begin to predict that every time you display physical romance, you want sex. You always want to keep your partner on edge and guessing. You can do this by mixing it up and sometimes going all the way and other times holding back and letting the passion build for a few days until you allow it to evolve into sexual romance.

Even if your partner likes physical romance, it doesn't mean they will like all physical touches. They may prefer some over others. Again, communication is the key to finding out what your partner likes. However, these are great places to start:

- Sensual massages
- Caressing or stroking
- Hugging
- Holding hands
- Cuddling or holding
- Kissing the face
- Kissing the lips

For Emotional People

For anyone who likes emotional intimacy, they will prefer acts of romance that stir up emotions inside of them. While physical touch will be one aspect of this, there are much more. In fact, in most cases, one of the other methods will be more likely to stir up the romance than physical touching will. Again, you want to use your actions as an opportunity to romance your partner whether you want to have sex or not. Especially with emotional people, using acts of romance only to have sex can lead to a greater sense of hurt feelings and it can actually heavily damage the intimacy between you and your partner, thus destroying the romance. If you want to succeed, you need to be willing to be romantic without sexual intentions on a regular basis, as well as romantic with sexual intentions from time to time.

If your partner likes emotional romance, you need to be certain that your romantic actions are always genuine. Those who are turned on by their emotions are often equally turned off by their emotions, and this can quickly destroy things in your relationship. Never commit an act of romance if it isn't genuinely coming from your heart. If you are, however, acting from your heart, the following ideas are a great place to start:

- Poetry
- Telling about how you feel
- Saying "I love you."
- Showing you care through words and actions
- Romantic gestures such as flowers or chocolate

- Remembering important things about them
- Looking into their eyes to establish emotional connection

Stirring up the romance in your relationship is important if you want to have a strong sex life. Before you start focusing on new sex positions and how to spice up sex itself, you want to build a strong foundation. A relationship that is strong with intimacy and romance is one where sex will be uninhibited and much more enjoyable for both parties. It is important that you put in the groundwork to ensure that your relationship is strong outside of sex if you want to have mind blowing sex that is incredible every single time.

Chapter 3

Different Types of Positions

There are two main types of sexual positions that the average couple uses in the bedroom. While other sex position books like Kama Sutras and similar texts will give you several types of positions, the various others are most often positions that are not easily accomplished by the average person. In other words, they are virtually useless to everyday couples who just want to have sex and don't want to have to learn different foot positioning's and balancing acts just to have it.

The two types of sex enjoyed by average couples include: sensual sex and spicy sex. Sensual sex is a more emotional experience, whereas spicy sex is a more physical experience. Despite each of them speaking to a unique, intimate preference, most individuals enjoy a mixture of both. Communicating with your partner to find out what they are comfortable with is the best way to ensure that you both enjoy the experience and that it brings you two closer together in the long run.

Sensual Sex

Sensual sex is typically a more emotional sexual experience. It is a love-making style of sex that invokes various emotions to help bring the two lovers closer together. It is as much emotional as it is physical. On a physical level, different sexual areas are being stimulated in a gentle manner that can bring each party to climax in a gentle sense. A large part of what brings about the climax, however, is the emotional addition. In sensual sex, there is a heightened sense of emotions that come into action.

The best way to heighten the experience of sensual sex is to include eye contact and use kinder and more romantic dirty talking. This is often where you will find couples saying "I love you" during sex. It is most often a slower experience that allows each moment to be enjoyed more thoroughly. As you may have expected, this type is most often favored by those who prefer emotional intimacy. Still, even those who prefer physical intimacy will enjoy the pleasures of sensual sex as well. For some who are extremely physical, however, too much sensual sex may not be stimulating enough and therefore not enjoyable on a regular basis.

Spicy Sex

Spicy sex is a more physical experience, and it can be anything from dirtier language and quicker movements to more physical actions such as spanking and clawing. There is no right or wrong way to have spicy sex with your partner. For those who prefer physical intimacy, they are more likely to feel connected to their partner through physical sex. While those who don't understand it may believe it to be rude or mean, those who prefer it find that it heightens the intimacy and romance between partners because it relies on trust and intuitively knowing each other's boundaries and preferences. In fact, because of this element of trust and intuitive knowing, many emotional romantics also have a unique passion for spicy sex, as well.

The best way to heighten the experience of spicy sex is to go with the flow. Do more of what your partner likes and less thinking overall.

You should seek as many ways to be physical with your partner as possible. You can be physical through the act of thrusting, as well as with your hands and, if you're creative enough, other body parts as well. Again, how far your partner likes to take it will be unique to them so always be sure to communicate and never go further than they like. If you do, you risk destroying the intimacy and romance between you and your partner, as well as trust and other important bonds.

Gender Preferences

When you are having sex with your partner, it is important that you never assume what they prefer based on their gender. Many men prefer sensual, sexual experiences and many females prefer physical. While it was often believed that men are more physical and female are more sensual, it has been found that preferences are individual and not gender-based. If you want to ensure that you and your partner both have mind-blowing experiences, you will want to communicate to learn what your partner prefers. Remember, despite their intimate and romantic preferences, they may prefer a style of sex that is different or unique to them. Learning this information gives you the best opportunity to ensure that they have a wonderful experience in the bedroom with you.

Chapter 4

Sensual Positions

Sensual positions are extremely emotional and generally come from a more loving place in the heart. Emotional romantics tend to love sensual positions as they allow them to get physical stimulation as well as emotional stimulation which heightens the experience and makes it even easier for them to have a mind-blowing orgasm. If your partner is an emotional romantic, you will want to include sensual sex in your experience. Remember, not every experience needs to be sensual and not every experience needs to be *only* sensual. It is perfectly okay and even normal to mix it up.

Many people feel as though sensual sex is only the missionary position, but this is not true. There are actually many different positions that can be sensual for you and your partner to enjoy together. While missionary is one of them, there are many others you can consider. The following 20 positions will add a sensual element to your sexual experience.

The Rocking Horse

This position is an elaborated version of the missionary style. It is a female-on-top position that allows the female partner to have near total control over the movements. This position allows both partners to lovingly gaze at each other or cuddle each other as they make love. Because of the set-up of the position, the man can also take over and have control over the movements as well.

Him: Put your arms out behind you and lean back on them as you sit up. Your legs can either be straight out in front of you, knees up, or crossed. If you are controlling the movement, you may want to have your knees bent for leverage, but otherwise sit however feels comfortable for you.

Her: Sit on top of your man with a leg on either side of his hips. You should be on your knees, using your shins as leverage to help you with movements. However, you can sit in any way that feels comfortable to you and your partner. From this position, you can cradle your man's head, look into his eyes, or even put his face on your chest if that feels comfortable.

The Slide

This is another girl-on-top position, but both partners are able to have more control over the movements in this one. Still, because of the position, the female will have slightly more control than the male when it comes to thrusting. This position is very close to missionary but has a slight twist on it which makes it have a unique feeling.

Him: You want to lie on your back with your legs out straight. Once your partner is on top of you, you can use your hands to caress her back or bum, or you can even hold her face and kiss her as she rides you.

Her: You want to lay down on top of your man, keeping your legs straight out as well. While you can sit in whatever position you like, the straighter you keep your legs, the more your g-spot will be stimulated with this position.

The Nirvana

This is a man-on-top variation of missionary that gives him a greater opportunity to reach the g-spot and bring her to climax. It also allows the partners to look into each other's eyes and have an emotional experience brought into the bedroom.

Her: You want to lay down on your back with your legs straight out. For the best g-spot action make sure that your thighs are pressed together, and you do not spread your legs.

Him: You should get on top of your partner now and put one knee on either side of her thighs, helping her keep her legs together. Then, enter her from the front. You can prop yourself up on your hands or elbows to help you from crushing her. From here you can look into her eyes, kiss her, or even cuddle your face into her neck.

The Padlock

This is a saucier position that is still easy for average couples to experience. It involves the use of a surface that is roughly waist-high for the male partner, so you can use your bed, a table, a countertop, or anything else that provides the right height for the male in the relationship.

Her: You want to sit on top of the waist-height surface and lean back on your arms. Once he has entered you, you can adjust your lean to find where it feels the best for you. If you want, you may wish to use a cushion or blanket underneath you so that it is less pressure on your tailbone and spine during this position. Once he enters you, you want to wrap your legs around him and lock your heels between his thighs.

Him: Once your partner has gotten comfortable on the surface, you want to lean in and enter her. You can use your hands behind her hips to help you get leverage for thrusting. She will then lock her feet between your thighs, so be sure to stand with your feet spread so she can create the "padlock."

The Ascent to Desire

While this may not be effective for all couples, it will be a wonderful position for couples where the male partner can easily lift the female partner. This position allows the female to develop a sense of trust in the male as he is holding her up and she must rely on him not to drop her. It is also an excellent position for maximizing g-spot and clitoral stimulation.

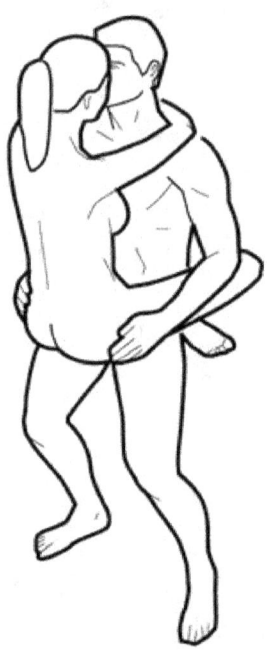

Him: You are simply going to stand and lift your partner up. You can use her thighs or bum to hold her so that you do not drop her. It may be easier to have her sitting on the bed or another waist-high surface at first so that you can enter her and lift her easier. Once she is lifted, you can begin thrusting.

Her: As he lifts you, use your arms to hold onto his shoulders. You can lean back slightly to maximize the pleasure you experience. Be sure to lean slowly so that you do not throw your man off balance! Let your legs swing freely with this one; it is all about relaxing into the pose for it to work.

The Suspender

This is another standing position where the man holds the female. This time, the position is slightly different, and the female is more responsible for holding herself up. Based on the structure of the position, it makes it easier for the female to orgasm from g-spot stimulation. It is also easier for the male to keep his balance and maximize the pleasure from the position.

Him: You are going to pick your lady up, rest her over you and then lean back against a wall. The support of the wall will help you keep your balance and will make thrusting significantly easier. You can hold your hands under her bum to help her keep her balance as you are thrusting.

Her: When he lifts you up, you are going to want to hold his shoulders or neck for support. If you want to get more energy out of the movement, you can put your feet on the wall behind him and push off of it for momentum. This will help build up the sensation of the position and make it more pleasurable for the both of you. It will also take some of the work off of him.

The Sexy Spoon

Simple spooning can be turned into passionate, romantic sex with the sexy spoon. This position allows you to cuddle while having sex. Because of the nature of this position, your bodies meld together perfectly making it a highly sensual position that can have an increased pleasure for both parties.

Her: This position is easiest for you. You simply want to lay on your side with your knees bent, so that your man can access you from behind. In essence, you are the "little spoon" in this position.

Him: You are going to be the big spoon, coming up with your girl from behind. You can cuddle her, just as you would in regular spooning, and then enter her from behind. If you want to increase her pleasure, put your knees together between her legs so that hers are spread apart. You can then hug her or cup her breasts while you thrust.

The Reverse Spoon

This reverse spoon position has both partners facing one another as you have sex. It is almost like a missionary on the side, only a little different. Both

lovers will need to put in the effort for the thrusting to work. It is a very sensual position that has you very close to one another, touching with virtually every part of your body.

Him: You are going to lay on your side facing your partner. You want to be leaning back slightly so that you can get leverage to thrust her. You can put a pillow behind your back for added support if the lean is too uncomfortable for you. Alternatively, your woman can put her leg behind your back and hold you up with her leg.

Her: You are going to mount your man from the side, putting your leg over his hip and behind his back. To help him out, you can put your knee down behind his back and use your leg to support him in the position. From there, you can cuddle him while you both move to thrust.

The Glowing Juniper

This position requires a little more flexibility, but it is still an incredibly comfortable position to enter. It is also highly enjoyable for many women as it helps the man hit directly on the g-spot, making penetration much more enjoyable. It also allows the man to enter deeper than other positions, meaning he will get maximum pleasure from this position, too.

Him: You are going to sit with your legs straight out in front of you, spread open so that your woman can lay between them. You are not in charge of the thrusting in this position, so this will be more of a pleasure pose for you.

Her: You are going to lay down with your back between your man's legs and your legs wrapped around either side of his chest. Your feet should be on the floor or bed behind your partner. Then, you can use your legs as leverage to push off of your man. This gives you full control over penetration depth and speed.

The Kneel

This face to face position is vertical, so both partners are upright. You are not standing for this position, however, which makes it a unique and fun pose to try out. Both partners get full control over motion and momentum, meaning that as much or as little energy can be put into the thrusting motions of the position.

Him: You are going to be sitting up on your knees, holding your lady in front of you.

Her: You are going to want to sit on your knees with one on either side of your man's thighs. Then, you can mount him and hug him as well as you both thrust.

The Rock N Roller

This position combines the pleasures of face to face positions and face to back positions. It is an extremely easy move to get into and can be done by virtually anyone. This position allows for her g-spot to be stimulated while he gains a deeper penetration.

Her: You are going to lay on your back with your legs in the air. Once your man gets into position, you will rest them on his shoulders. You can use a pillow under your head as well as under your tailbone if you need extra support to keep this position comfortable for you. The pillow under the tailbone can also make it easier for your man to get deeper penetration.

Him: You are going to scoot in and enter your lady while she puts her legs over your shoulders. This position will put you in total control so you can go as deeply as you want and you control the movement.

Always be sure to start slowly and move at her pace, as entering too deeply too quickly can cause pain and ruin the moment for you two.

The Amazon

This position is a simple position that involves a chair and allows you and your partner to gain a deeper entry and a great sensual experience. It is a woman-on-top position that gives her the most control over the movement, but he can contribute if he wants to as well.

Him: You are going to sit on a chair with your knees out in front of you and your feet flat on the floor. When she mounts you, you can hug her, hold her bum to gain some control over the movements and help her out, or you can place them anywhere else that feels comfortable and natural for you.

Her: You are going to mount your man, putting one leg on either side of the chair. You will want to have your feet planted firmly on the floor as this is what will give you leverage for your position. You can hug him or place your hands wherever feels comfortable. If you need more leverage to help with movement, you might consider holding the back of the chair and using your arms to help pull you up with each bounce.

The Super 8

This is a spiced up version of the traditional missionary position. It is an extremely easy man-on-top position that adds pleasure and comfort to the experience. Because of the position's structure, it allows for maximum eye-gazing and sensuality to be added to the experience.

Her: You are going to lay on your back on the bed, using a pillow under your head for comfort if need be. When your man mounts you, you can then wrap your legs behind his knees so that he can get a deeper penetration.

Him: You are going to mount your lady like you would missionary style, only instead of having your legs around hers, they are going to be between hers. You can then rest up on your hands so that you are well above her, allowing you to gaze into her eyes while you are thrusting.

Curled Up

This position is like a variation of the Rock N Roller. You are going to get the best of both face to face and face to back facing positions, allowing you the opportunity to get deeper penetration and sensual eye-gazing in. Of course, from the nature of this position it has maximum g-spot action, so you can guarantee that both are going to get great pleasure from this position!

Her: You are going to lay on your back with your legs up in the air. When your man mounts you, you want to put your feet on his chest, curling your knees up into your chest. This position takes away virtually all of your control over the movement but allows for deep entry and great g-spot stimulation.

Him: You are going to scoot up behind your girl and enter her as though you are entering her from behind. When you do, she will put her feet on your chest. You can then put your hands next to her shoulders and thrust at your own free will. Remember, she does not have any control in this position so listen to her cues to ensure that the position is enjoyable for both of you.

The Proposal

This position gives a whole new purpose to getting down on one knee. Only with this position, you are both getting down on one knee. It may be awkward for some, but for those who can get into this position and maximize movements, they will gain significant amounts of pleasure from this position.

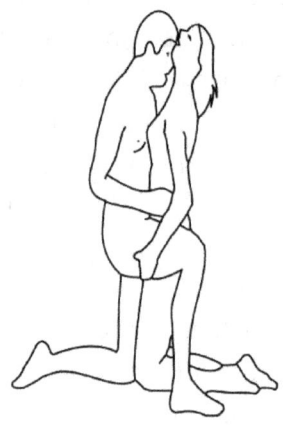

Him: You are going to get down on one knee. When she gets down in front of you, you can cup her bum to get more control over the movement. While she will have control over this movement, it will primarily be you who is getting the thrusting action in. She will be rocking her hips to meet your thrusts.

Her: Get down on one knee in front of your man, with the same knee forward. It should result in each of you having one leg up next to each other's hip on the same side. You should put your foot on the other side of his shin so that you can get a good locking action going between your bodies. Hug him for support, and as he thrusts, you can rock your hips to meet his action.

Blossoming Lotus

This is a sitting down position that looks a lot like sitting cross-legged. It is a female-on-top position, and because of the angle the man's legs will be at, the female must take control on this one. It is a very

pleasurable position and allows the lady to choose penetration depth and speed.

Him: You are going to sit down with your ankles crossed on the ground. If the pressure of someone on your lap hurts your ankles, you can also sit with the bottoms of your feet touching.

Her: You are going to mount your man and sit with your feet behind him. This position relies more on rocking than on bouncing, so you can touch the bottoms of your feet together as well if it is comfortable. Find the position that feels natural to you that allows you to rock back and forth while still getting enough pleasure from the position.

The Sphinx

This is a position that allows the man to enter from the back. It is a highly pleasurable position that gives the woman the opportunity to have control in the movements as well. While she will likely not take full control, she can rock her hips back to meet each thrust.

Her: Start by sitting on your hands and knees. Then, squat your pelvis to the bed and bend your arms so that you are resting on your forearms. You should look as though you are in the same pose as a sphinx. When he thrusts you, you can rock your hips back to meet his movements.

Him: You can enter like you are in doggy position, or you can lay with your legs straight out behind you and thrust that way. Lay in any way that feels most comfortable to you for this position. You have the most control so that penetration will be up to you for this one.

The Side Kick

This is another position that allows the man to enter from the back and gives him full control over movements. It is a very sensual pose that is highly relaxing for the female. This position allows great clitoris stimulation and is easy for the man to get leverage on the thrusting as well.

Her: You want to lay on your stomach with your legs straight out. You can also bend one knee up to the side if you prefer, as this will give you added clitoris stimulation. This position is meant to be relaxing for you, so there is not much you need to do, besides relax completely into the position.

Him: You are going to come up behind your lady on your knees, entering her from behind. You can hold her hip so that you get more leverage on thrusting, which will give you the ability to penetrate at any depth or speed you desire. You can also practice moving your hips around a little so that you gain g-spot stimulation as well, maximizing her pleasure from this position.

The Waterfall

This position does require balance and flexibility, but it can be highly sensual and extremely stimulating when done correctly. The waterfall is a woman-on-top position that requires the man to make all of the efforts in thrusting

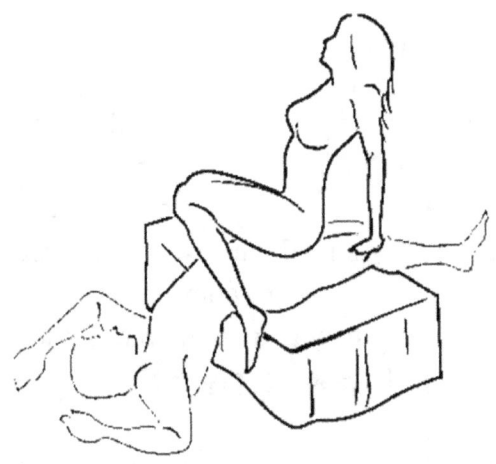

Him: You are going to sit on a chair with your knees out in front of you. When your lady mounts you, you are going to hold her back to allow her to lay back on your legs. You will need to support her to ensure she doesn't fall during this position. Once she is laying back, you can begin to thrust.

Her: You are going to mount your man like you do in the Amazon pose, but this time you are going to lay back over his lap and pull your knees up in the air.

Your entire body should be completely supported by his, giving him total control over the movements in this position.

The Right Angle

This is an extremely easy position that gives great stimulation and pleasure to both parties. It can be accomplished by anyone and can be done virtually anywhere in your home or anywhere else. Additionally, you can customize this position to maximize pleasure by giving different stimulation to various areas of the sexual organs.

Her: You are going to lay back on any surface that is roughly waist-high for your man. If there isn't one, you can lay on any surface that would be waist-high if he were on his knees. When he enters you, you can put your feet on his chest, your legs over his shoulders, your legs around his back, or anywhere else that feels comfortable for you.

Him: You are going to enter your girl from between her legs. Depending on what surface she is on, you may be able to stand, or you may have to go down on your knees. If you are on your knees, you might consider putting a pillow beneath them for added support and comfort. You will get a full body view of her, so you can gaze in all of her beauty while thrusting.

Chapter 5

Spicy Positions

For couples who are into spicier sex positions, we have compiled a list of 20 of the best spicy positions as well. These positions are fiery than the sensual positions and allow for more physical action. They will still be highly stimulating but will allow for a saucier edge to be added.

These are for people who adore physical intimacy, or for those who enjoy trying out the wild side once in a while. Remember, before you try anything that may be considered kinky, you want to talk to your partner first.

It is always a good idea to make sure that they would be interested in the act as well to ensure that both parties enjoy the experience and no intimacy is lost from lack of communication!

The Pretzel Dip

The pretzel dip is a unique pose that requires an interlacing of legs to get into position. It allows for maximum pleasure based on the position as penetration will cause the man to stimulate various areas of the vagina that are not normally directly stimulated during sex. This position allows you to get deeper penetration than you do in missionary style while still enjoying the pleasure of looking into each other's eyes during sex.

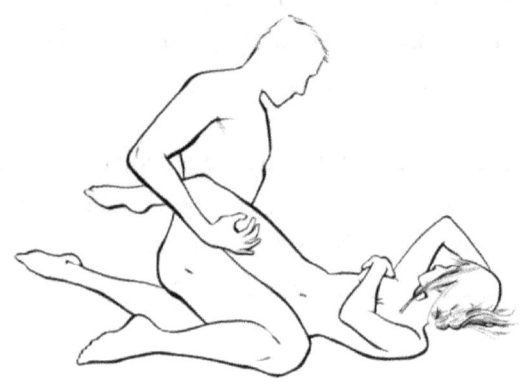

Her: You are going to lay on your side, with your legs spread open so that your man can enter you from between them. When he does, you will wrap your knee around his hip, allowing you to get balance. If you need, you can put a pillow or support behind your back so that it's easier for you to stay upright.

Him: You want to enter your girl from between her legs so that her top leg can wrap around your hips.

Then, you can enter her and thrust from that position. Because your hands are not as needed, you can use them to stimulate her nipples or clitoris.

Face Off

This position involves the man sitting on the edge of the bed so that the lady can be on top and take control. It is similar to the sensual pose "The Amazon," but allows for the lady to get more leverage so she can gain deeper penetration and greater speed.

Him: You want to sit on the edge of the bed with your feet planted firmly on the floor. This won't work on a chair but may work on another surface like a counter or the couch. When she mounts you, you can hold her bum for added control, or you can simply wrap your hands behind her and let her control the movements.

Her: You are going to mount your man and keep your knees on either side of his hips. You want to keep your shins down on the surface, and your toes curled under so that you can have maximum control over movements.

This will give you the opportunity to control the depth of penetration and speed of movements. You can wrap your hands behind his shoulders to help with added support and momentum.

Cowgirl's Helper

This is similar to the position known as "Cowgirl" which is highly popular but works slightly differently. The position allows for maximum penetration, and movements, all whilst giving the girl total control. Because of the structure, however, she gains a significant amount of support from her lover.

Him: You want to lay on your back with your knees propped up. They shouldn't be too high, but high enough that they can support your lady while she rides you. You can use your hands to help her with the movements as well by tucking them under her bum.

Her: You want to mount your man so that you are face to face, but you should be sitting upright. Place your hands on his chest and use this as an opportunity to support yourself as you rock yourself back and forth on him.

You can slide your bum up and down his propped up legs for maximum support which will allow you to maintain your energy for a lot longer than a traditional Cowgirl pose.

Leap Frog

This is similar to a doggy style pose but allows for deeper penetration and greater pleasure for both. It is a man-in-control pose, but the woman can add some effort into the movements as well.

Because of the female's position, she can also use her own hands to stimulate her clitoris during penetration.

Her: You are going to prop yourself up on your knees and then fold over so that your chest is on the bed. With your free hands you can play with yourself, or simply get comfortable and relax into the experience.

Him: You are going to enter your girl from behind just like it is doggy style. You should be on your knees to gain entry, and you can use your hands on her hips to help you get leverage to penetrate more effectively.

Ballet Dancer

This is a standing pose in which both partners are standing. This pose allows for both of you to be face to face while still adding a sexy benefit to the position.

Additionally, it does not take a significant amount of either party's energy so it can be enjoyed for a lot longer than other standing poses.

Him: You want to stand with both feet on the ground so that you can keep your balance in the position. You are going to be the anchor, so it is important that you keep your balance or else you will both fall over. When your lady puts her leg up, you should hook your hand underneath it to support her leg so that she does not tire quickly. This will allow for you to stay in the position much longer. Your other hand can support her back.

Her: You want to stand in front of your man and throw one leg up over his waist. He will support it with his hand so that you do not have to hang it in a balancing act. Then, he can enter you and start thrusting. You can hold his shoulders for added balance, and so that you can contribute to the movement.

Cowgirl

The cowgirl is a highly popular pose that is a woman-on-top position that allows for the man to lay back and relax while his lady takes control. It can be enjoyed as a slower and more sensual position, or it can be rocked to offer an extremely sexy and steamy lady-in-control situation.

Him: You are going to lay on your back in any way that is comfortable for you. You can have your knees up to help support your lady, or you can have them down flat if you prefer. You can use your free hands to stimulate her clitoris or nipples, or you can simply relax into the position and let her be the boss for this one.

Her: You are going to mount your man and ride him from the top. You can squat over him and bounce for movement, or you can put your knees down on the bed and use that for leverage. Switch it up between the two to see what helps you gain momentum and get the best ride.

Corkscrew

This position requires you to be near the edge of your bed. It allows you both to contribute to the work required to make this position effective and provides incredible stimulation as well.

Her: You are going to bend over the bed and put one leg up on the bed next to you. You can then squeeze your thighs together so that you can meet your man's tempo to make the move even more enjoyable and keep him from having to do all of the work.

Him: You are going to want to mount your girl from behind by keeping one leg on the floor and putting one leg up on the bed. If you want to take complete control, you can tuck your leg under hers so that she is "locked" into place. Then you can ride her like you would in any doggy style-type position.

Wheelbarrow

This position requires some upper body strength from both parties, as it will rely on your arms to keep the position from collapsing. The position requires a little bit of work to get into, but once you are in it, it is an incredible position for pleasure and stimulation for both parties.

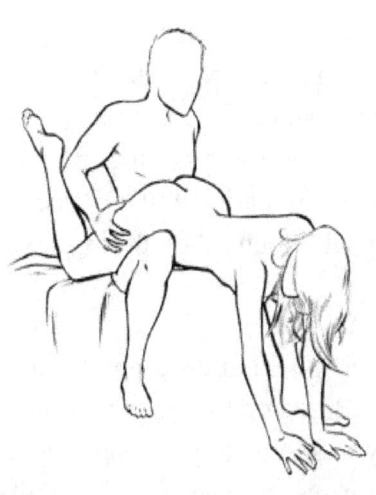

Her: You want to get on your hands and knees as though you are going to enter a doggy position. However, your man is going to lift up your back end so you want to make sure that you can hold your weight with your arms before he picks you up. When he does pick you up you, want to wrap your legs around his bum so that you can stay in position.

Him: You are going to lift your lady up from the back, and she will wrap her legs around you. You can then hold onto her hips to keep her in position and prevent her from dropping. From this position, you can enter her and start thrusting.

X-Factor

This position is coined because both of your bodies together will look like an "x" from an aerial view. It is a pleasurable position for both parties because it allows the penetration to come in at a unique angle which means that stimulation will be directly in areas that are not typically focused on during sex.

Her: You want to lay on your back and get comfortable. This position does not require a lot of work from you. Based on the position, you won't get the opportunity to stimulate your vagina in any way, but you can always go ahead and stimulate your nipples instead, or simply caress your man's back.

Him: You want to mount your woman by laying on top of her at an angle to where she is. Your bodies should look like an "x" when they are fit together. You can then enter her and thrust at any tempo you desire.

The Caboose

This is an upright spooning style position that allows him to enter you from the back. It allows for closeness while still allowing for deep and stimulating penetration that makes the move highly desirable. It is great for people who like to kiss and bite on the neck.

Him: You are going to sit with your knees bent and spread so that your lady can fit in between you. You will want to put at least one hand out behind you to take some of your weight so that you can leverage your position to allow you to thrust into her.

Her: You want to sit on his lap as though you are recreating a spooning position only sitting upright. You should fit directly between his legs so that you are both comfortable in the position. He can then cuddle you from behind while you both move to make the action happen.

Reverse Cowgirl

This is a popular position, and it provides great stimulation, deep penetration, and the opportunity for the girl to be in control. It is popular for a reason!

Him: You want to lay on your back with your legs straight out. You can have a pillow under your head for comfort, and to help you get a better view of your lady's body.

Her: You are going to mount your man so that he gets a full view of your back. You can put your hands on his thighs to help you get leverage for movement.

Stand and Deliver

This is a stand-up position that takes complete control away from the lady and gives it to the man. It is great for deep penetration and maximum stimulation.

Her: You are going to stand in front of your man and bend over. When you are bent over, he will grab your hands, and then you can bend further forward. You want to be folded forward as far as possible as this will give control away to the man. It also allows him to get deeper.

Him: You are going to grab her by the hands and let her fold over forward. Then you can enter her from behind and penetrate her as deep and hard as you want. This gives you total control over tempo and depth.

Scoop Me Up

This is essentially the spooning position but has the female leaning forward a little more so that the man can get better control over the position. It is meant to be comfortable and relaxing while also stimulating and spicy. Because of all of the free hands you can add stimulation to various parts of each other's body for added effect.

Her: You are going to be the little spoon. You want to lay on your side with a pillow under you. You can lean forward slightly so that you are resting on your belly. If you need to, you can put your top knee forward to make it more comfortable for you.

Him: You will come up behind your girl and ride her from the back. You will be the big spoon in this position. You are going to have the most control over this position, but she can move backward to meet your thrusts so that you both enjoy it.

Reverse Scoop

This is a face to face position that will give you both the opportunity to have maximum stimulation and pleasure while also getting a sensual and romantic aspect added. It is easy and allows both parties to have control over the movements.

Her: You are going to face your man and lay with your legs close together, you want to get into a position that will allow you to gain some control in the movement and enjoy yourself.

Him: You are going to meet your girl by scooting up to face her. You can spread your legs around her and mount her from the front, or you can go between her legs. You want to enter her from any position that feels comfortable for you to gain maximum tempo.

Magic Mountain

Magic Mountain is a sitting position that allows both partners to face each other. It is a more advanced position that will spice up your bedroom life and add a sense of creativity to your sexual encounters. It is not necessarily a great position for deep penetration, but it certainly adds maximum stimulation to the g-spot!

Him: You are going to sit on your bum with your hands behind you to lean back on. Then, you want to bend your legs so that your knees are up and your feet are flat on the floor.

Her: You are going to sit the same as your partner is with your knees up and leaning back on your hands. However, you want to put your legs on your partner's hips so that they are back near his hands and you are on "top" in this position.

The Chairman

The chairman is a unique position where the male partner sits on the edge of the bed, and the female partner sits on top of him. It is a back to face position that allows for him to enter from the back and both partners to get deep penetration and great stimulation. It may take some practice to get into, but once you are in it, it is highly enjoyable.

Him: You are going to sit on the edge of the bed with one foot on the floor and one on the bed. The foot on the floor will be used to leverage your thrusting, so you want to make sure your foot is firmly planted on the floor.

Her: You are going to sit on you man with one foot on the floor. You can use this foot to help leverage so that you both contribute to the tempo of the thrusting. This will provide maximum pleasure for both partners.

Cowboy

The cowboy is very similar to the cowgirl but is a man-on-top position. It allows for great pleasure and g-spot stimulation, as well as clitoris stimulation. The tighter her legs are pressed together, the more pleasurable it will be for both.

Her: You are going to lay on your back with your legs straight out. You can bend them slightly, but you want to keep them as straight as possible so that your man can get a comfortable perch on top of you.

Him: You are going to mount your girl on top just like she would in cowgirl position. You want to have one leg on either side of her hips and enter her from the top. You can gain maximum leverage any way you want to get the most pleasure from the experience.

Golden Arches

This is similar to a magic mountain, except that the man's legs are more relaxed and he has greater control over the movement in the pose. You both get a wonderful full-body view of each other, and the female can get great clitoris action from free hands.

Him: You are going to sit down and lean back on your hands. You want to keep your legs relatively straight out in front of you.

Her: You are going to get on top of your man and put one leg on either side of his hips. You want to lean back on your hands and ride him from the top. You will have the most control in this position, so it is up to you to take over the tempo.

The Seashell

This position requires the female to be fairly flexible, but it can be modified to reduce the flexibility requirements if necessary. It is a great position for deep penetration as well as clitoris stimulation.

Her: You are going to lay on your back with your legs in the air. When your man mounts you, he is going to push your legs forward towards your chest so you can get comfortable into the pose. It allows for your clitoris to be stimulated by the movement as well as your g-spot to be stimulated by the angle of penetration.

Him: You are going to enter your girl, and her legs will be rested upon your chest. You can then lean forward to push her legs into her own chest so that she is folded in half. Always go slow so that your lady can stop you when it becomes uncomfortable for her. You can then control the tempo and depth of the position.

Butter Churner

This position is a man-on-top position where the female is required to be flexible. The man will be on top and can have control over tempo, depth, and angle of penetration. It can be customized in any way you desire to gain maximum enjoyment from the position.

Her: You are going to lay on your back and then put your legs up and fold them over so that your knees are up by your head. You should be resting upon your shoulders, and you can use your hands out behind you to keep your balance in this position.

Him: You are going to sit on top of your lady and put your foot on either side of your woman. Then, you can enter her and choose your own depth, tempo, and angle. You can stand in any direction to change the penetration angle if you desire.

Chapter 6

Beyond the Bedroom

There are many ways to spice up your sex life, and as you learned there is a lot beyond the bedroom that can be done to enhance it as well. This chapter will explore some ideas of what you can do to make your sex life even better outside of the bedroom.

Do Fun Things Together

Doing fun things together allows you to increase your dopamine levels together as well. When you have fun together, it increases your closeness with one another and can enhance the joy you experience with each other. It adds a unique sense of intimacy to your relationship that cannot be added by sexual experiences.

Ideally, you want to have fun together in a way that gets your blood pumping and your adrenaline rushing. Going to an amusement park, ice skating, visiting an upbeat concert, or otherwise doing something fun and exciting can increase the happiness of your experience with one another. Having fun this way can add an energy to your relationship that will carry into the bedroom and make sex even more enjoyable.

Kiss More Often

Many couples, especially those who have been together a while tend to kiss less often. Kissing is a highly romantic and passionate act and should be done regularly. Think about it, at the beginning of the relationship you likely kissed your partner a lot more frequently than you do now that you are more comfortable together. You want to start doing it more often.

When you are kissing more regularly, don't just increase the volume but also increase the passion in each kiss. There is no need to peck and go. Give the kiss a few moments and truly experience your partner with each kiss. You can include your hands and body as well, or even kiss in other intimate areas such as on the cheek, forehead or hand.

Recall What It Was Like to Meet

When you first met you likely spent a lot more time getting to know one another and a lot less time watching TV or doing other things to pass the time.

You can spend some time asking each other questions about life, or even just reminisce on the days when you met each other. Getting to know each other all over again is a great way to rekindle the flame in a relationship.

The reality is that we don't all stay the same in life. Throughout your relationship, you and your partner will change several times over. Their preferences for certain things may change, and these are all great things to learn about each other all over again as you rekindle your love by communicating and asking questions.

Describe Your Sexual Fantasies

Many times, sex is just about the act and couples don't really speak a lot about sex outside of the bedroom. A great way to spark up a flame and add passion to your sex life is to talk about each other's fantasies and interests. This gives you an opportunity to get to know each other's sexual preferences more intimately which means that you can gain maximum enjoyment out of sex. It allows you to have a better idea of what your partner likes and what they don't like, and how you can make sexual experiences more enjoyable for them.

Keep The Mystery Alive

In relationships, it can be easy to get to know each other so intimately that there appears to be no mystery left in the relationship anymore. This can be counterproductive to the process of bringing romance back into your relationship. A lot of romance builds around mystery and the desire to know each other more intimately than you presently do. There are many ways that you can add mystery back into your relationship, even if you already know almost everything about each other. Using sentences that add mystery, clothes that spark intrigue and even simple texts that make the other partner wonder what you have planned for the evening can help add mystery back into the relationship.

When the mystery is present, the other person wonders about you. They start thinking about you and may even become obsessed with wanting to know what you have planned because they are curious. Curiosity is the key to creating mystery and getting your partner wondering about you and what you have to offer them that is unique from before.

Express Gratitude

A great way to help your partner feel cared for and show them how much they mean to you is to express your gratitude. Expressing gratitude takes very little time but can have a significant impact on the quality of your relationship. When people feel cared for and loved, they want to show more care and love to the one they feel for as well.

This can increase the quality of your relationship, making you both feel more appreciated.

In relationships, the little things often get overlooked. People forget that the little things count and so they don't take the time to show appreciation and gratitude for them genuinely. Something as simple as "I really appreciate that you always support me in my decisions" or "I really appreciate that you make me breakfast each morning" can go a long way. Even though repeat activities can lead to things being expected, it is always good to show that you don't necessarily expect things to be done for you or in a certain way. Always show that you care about what your partner does in life and for you, as this will increase the quality of your time together and make you both feel more loved overall. When you feel more loved, the sparks will naturally fly in your relationship.

Don't Hold Grudges

Holding grudges can destroy relationships really quickly. When people hold grudges, they fail to let go of things that are no longer relevant, and it can lead to destruction in the relationship. You may feel that if you let go, it shows your partner that their mistake was acceptable, and for you, it may seem like you are allowing them to do it again. In reality, when you let it go, you are giving them permission to be human and make mistakes. It allows them the opportunity to see what they've done and make a change, knowing that you will appreciate the change wholeheartedly. It never pays to hold a grudge in your relationship.

Care About Self Care

How you care about yourself and how your partner cares about themselves is important when it comes to having a healthy relationship. A healthy relationship almost always leads to a healthy sex life, since your sex life is so closely linked to the health of your relationship. It is important that you both emphasize on self-care and take the time to truly nurture your own needs before nurturing your partner's. Yes, before. You cannot pour out of an empty cup, and keeping your cup empty is not a favor to your partner. Instead, it is a drawback that will lead to your relationship falling apart.

Taking care of your own self can come in many ways. You should look towards developing a healthy relationship with yourself if you want to really get serious about self-care. Take yourself on dates, have alone time, and get to know yourself more. The added benefit of getting to know yourself more is that you learn things about yourself that you may not have known before. You can share these things with your spouse, thus expanding your realm of conversation topics and letting you continue to get to know each other, even long after the relationship has worn out its honeymoon phase.

There are many ways that you can spark romance back into your relationship outside of the bedroom. By having these types of activities present in your day-to-day life, you increase the amount of romance and intimacy that lies between you and your partner and it causes for you both to become more eager about your sex life. A relationship that is rich outside of the bedroom is one that will be exciting inside of the bedroom.

When you are looking to cause sparks outside of the bedroom, you want to take your time and really get to know one another. Forget everything you've learned up until now and take the time to learn again. In many cases what you know now can be relevant but may no longer be the whole truth. People regularly change, and this can lead to there being a disconnection between what you are thinking and what your partner is wanting. By communicating, you can alleviate this disconnection and create a renewed sense of appreciation and romance between yourself and your partner.

Overall, the best thing you can do for your sex life is to nurture all areas of your relationship. The more successful your relationship is elsewhere, the more exciting your sex life will be. It creates a sense of deep knowing and trust that cannot be faked between two people. When this trust and love is present, the sex you experience will be unlike anything you have ever had before. Even relationships that have been alive for a long time can benefit from this type of rekindling.

Conclusion

Thank you so much for reading through.

Before you go, I'd like to say "thank you" for purchasing my book.

I know you could have picked from dozens of books on Sex Positions, but you took a chance with my guide.

So a big thanks for downloading this book and reading all the way to the end.

Now, I'd like to ask for a *small* favor. Could you please take a minute or two and leave a review for this book on Amazon?

This feedback will help me continue to write the kind of Books that will help you get results. And if you loved it, then please let me know :-)

You can also follow me on Twitter @bambicolt

www.ingramcontent.com/pod-product-compliance
Lightning Source LLC
Chambersburg PA
CBHW052116070526
44584CB00017B/2519